Our Auntie ("Tee-Tee") Uses a Chair with Wheels

Shonda McLaughlin, PhD, CRC

Archway Publishing books may be ordered through booksellers or by contacting:

Archway Publishing
1663 Liberty Drive
Bloomington, IN 47403
www.archwaypublishing.com
844-669-3957

Because of the dynamic nature of the Internet, any web addresses or links contained
in this book may have changed since publication and may no longer be valid. The views
expressed in this work are solely those of the author and do not necessarily reflect the
views of the publisher, and the publisher hereby disclaims any responsibility for them.

Any people depicted in stock imagery provided by Getty Images are models,
and such images are being used for illustrative purposes only.
Certain stock imagery © Getty Images.

ISBN: 978-1-6657-0783-1 (sc)
ISBN: 978-1-6657-0782-4 (hc)
ISBN: 978-1-6657-0784-8 (e)

Print information available on the last page.

Archway Publishing rev. date: 07/06/2021

Dedication

This book is dedicated to anyone who appreciate diversity in thoughts and in families.

I dedicate this book to my nieces, nephews, family, parents, siblings, and, of course, to the young and curious minds, especially those in rural areas.

Thanks, Ja'Mia, Ja'Nia, Linda, Derwin, the disability and military communities, those that I have served, and those who have taught me.

You all made this book possible.

List of Illustrations

1. Image of Ja'Nia and Ja'Mia swinging

2. Image of Tee-Tee working

3. Image of Tee-Tee and Ja'Mia cheering

4. Image of Tee-Tee, Ja'Mia, and Ja'Nia painting

5. Image of Tee-Tee, Ja'Nia, and Ja'Mia riding in Tee-Tee's wheelchair

6. Image of Tee-Tee, Ja'Mia, and Ja'Nia dancing and singing

7. Image of Ja'Mia and Ja'Nia laughing and playing hide-n-seek with Tee-Tee

8. Image of Tee-Tee, Ja'Mia, and Ja'Nia swinging

Acknowledgements

Along with my nieces and nephews, there are so many others that need acknowledgement for their invaluable relationships, time, lessons, motivation, and unwavering encouragement. They include:

Mr. Kenneth L. Bennett, Ms. Alfie D. Lingo-Armstrong, Dr. Allison Butler, Mr. Roger Deason, Mr. Evans Appiah, Mr. Gregory Barber, Mr. Ashraf Mohamed, Mrs. May and Ladys Agurto, and their children, Lucas, Liam, and Logan, Dr. Steve Zappalla, Mr. Herbert Morris, Mr. Steve Hardin, Mr. Kwabena Boateng and his family, Mr. David Lainez, Ms. Angela Perry, Ms. Danita Hill, Mr. Lavern Sellers, Mr. Tyler Coffie, Mr. & Mrs. Josh and Nit Hu, Ms. Lauren Clark, Ms. Michelle Williams, Mr. Jamison Smith,

Ms. Biljana Milenkovic and the team at DC Public Library-Friendship Heights, Ms. Zakiya Pettit, Ms. Aukima Benjamin,

Mr. and Mrs. Ian and Anne McIntosh, and their daughter Grace,

Ms. Michelle Brito and her daughter, Carmen, Ms. Diane Coleman and Not Dead Yet,

Ms. Kindra Mizell, Ms. Monica Tolliver,

Ms. Laurie Hansen, and my students and Graduate team of the Human Services Department at Purdue University Global.

THANK YOU!

Our names are Ja'Mia and Ja'Nia. We are sisters. And we want to tell you about our family...

...One of our aunties, "Tee-Tee," does not walk like us. She uses a chair with wheels, a "wheelchair," as she calls it, to get around. But, somehow, she still does things like everyone else. For instance, she is not only a professor, but she also serves Veterans and their spouses.

Tee-Tee works a lot, but she plays and has fun with us, too. For example, Tee-Tee attends games and cheers with and for us.

At times, we draw and paint together.

Sometimes, she allows us to ride in her chair with her. If we ask, she lets us blow the horn on her chair. She always says, "Don't forget that my chair is not a toy. It's how I get around."

Plus, we sing and dance together.

Surprisingly, Tee-Tee even plays hide-n-seek with us, but she NEVER wins. She is not good at hiding her wheels on her chair!

Those are just some of the things our Tee-Tee does. She does a lot more.

Do you have anyone in your family who uses a chair with wheels? What do you all do for fun?

Yes, our Tee-Tee uses a chair with wheels, a "wheelchair," but that does not matter... because she LOVES US!

The End.

Notes

Reader's Guide

The purpose of this book is to simplify a discussion regarding the inclusion and discussion of disability among the family and with friends. Below are some further questions/comments to continue the conversation.

1. We are all different as individuals and within our families. In what ways are you unique from your family members (i.e., family, brothers, sisters, cousins, etc.)?

2. Describe some of the similarities of Ja'Mia and Ja' Nia's family and yours?

3. Please share what you learned about Tee-Tee or from the book in general.

Printed in the United States
by Baker & Taylor Publisher Services